Heart on Fire

Susan B. Anthony Votes for President

Ann Malaspina

illustrated by Steve James

Albert Whitman & Company
Chicago, Illinois

To Rob, who always reminds me to vote.—*A.M.*

For Erma.—*S. J.*

Special thanks to Barbara Chapman, Jim Dierks, Thomas F. Ferrarese, Catherine Gilbert, Ann Gordon, Kathy Gustyn, Colleen Hurst, Doug Jones, Douglas A. Kellner, Ruth Rosenberg-Naparstek, Lori Slater, Susan Washington, and the volunteers at the Susan B. Anthony House in Rochester, New York.

Library of Congress Cataloging-in-Publication Data

Malaspina, Ann, 1957-
Heart on fire : Susan B. Anthony votes for president / by Ann Malaspina ; illustrated by Steve James.
p. cm.
ISBN 978-0-8075-3188-4 (hardcover)
1. Anthony, Susan B. (Susan Brownell), 1820-1906—Trials, litigation, etc. 2. Trials (Political crimes and offenses)—New York (State)—Juvenile literature. 3. Election law—New York (State)—Criminal provisions. 4. Women—Suffrage—United States—History—19th century—Juvenile literature. I. James, Steve. II. Title.
KF223.A58M35 2012
324.6'23092—dc23
[B]
2011034179

The design is by Nick Tiemersma.

For more information about Albert Whitman & Company,
visit our web site at www.albertwhitman.com.

The Fourteenth Amendment
Passed by Congress June 13, 1866
Ratified July 9, 1868

Section 1: All persons born or naturalized in the United States, and subject to the jurisdiction thereof, are citizens of the United States and of the State wherein they reside. No State shall make or enforce any law which shall abridge the privileges or immunities of citizens of the United States; nor shall any State deprive any person of life, liberty, or property, without due process of law; nor deny to any person within its jurisdiction the equal protection of the laws.

Section 5: The Congress shall have the power to enforce, by appropriate legislation, the provisions of this article.

The Nineteenth Amendment
Passed by Congress June 4, 1919
Ratified August 18, 1920

Section 1: The right of citizens of the United States to vote shall not be denied or abridged by the United States or by any State on account of sex.

Section 2: Congress shall have power to enforce this article by appropriate legislation.

Rochester, New York, November 1, 1872

Four days to the presidential election.
"Register now!" the morning paper said.
Susan B. Anthony jumped up
to grab her purse and wrap.

Out the door
and down the street
she flew.
Her sister Hannah and friend Mary
hoisted their skirts to keep up.

Women couldn't be equal to men
if they did not vote.
Miss Anthony's heels
tapped faster and faster.

At the voter registration office,
she marched in like a gust of wind.

This was the moment
Miss Anthony had dreamed of
for so long.
She demanded to
register to vote.

The inspectors looked up,
shocked
and confused.

Only men could sign up to vote.
Not women who owned property,
paid taxes,
held a job,
or raised children.
No woman was
allowed to cast a ballot.

Outrageous.
Unbelievable.
True.

Miss Anthony believed
women *did* have
the right to vote,
because of a new law,
the Fourteenth Amendment
to the Constitution.
All persons born
in the United States
have the same rights
as citizens,
she told the men.

Wasn't she a person—
and a citizen?

The inspectors scratched their heads.
They argued . . .
Yes, Miss Anthony's right!
debated . . .
No, women can't vote!
and disagreed.
Finally, one man said,
"Sign here."

It was done.
Miss Anthony had registered to vote.

Election Day, November 5, 1872

Up at dawn, Miss Anthony raced
to the polls at seven A.M. sharp.

Lighting the match,
Miss Anthony cast her vote.
Throwing more tinder,
fifteen other women voted, too.

That night before she slept,
she wrote her good friend Elizabeth Cady Stanton,
"Well I have been & gone & done it!!"

Miss Anthony had voted for president.
Trouble was simmering.

November 18, 1872

RAP-RAP-RAP.
The deputy federal marshal
stepped into the parlor
and took off his beaver hat.
What had he come for?
"To arrest you," he said, turning red.
Miss Anthony held out her hands.
"I demand that I should be arrested properly."
But he would not handcuff a lady.

At the federal office downtown,
she saw her sisters,
her friends who voted,
even the men who let them vote.
All arrested, too.

The charge:
*Voting without having
the lawful right to vote.*

Then she was sent home to wait.

No one could hear
her burning heart
pounding.

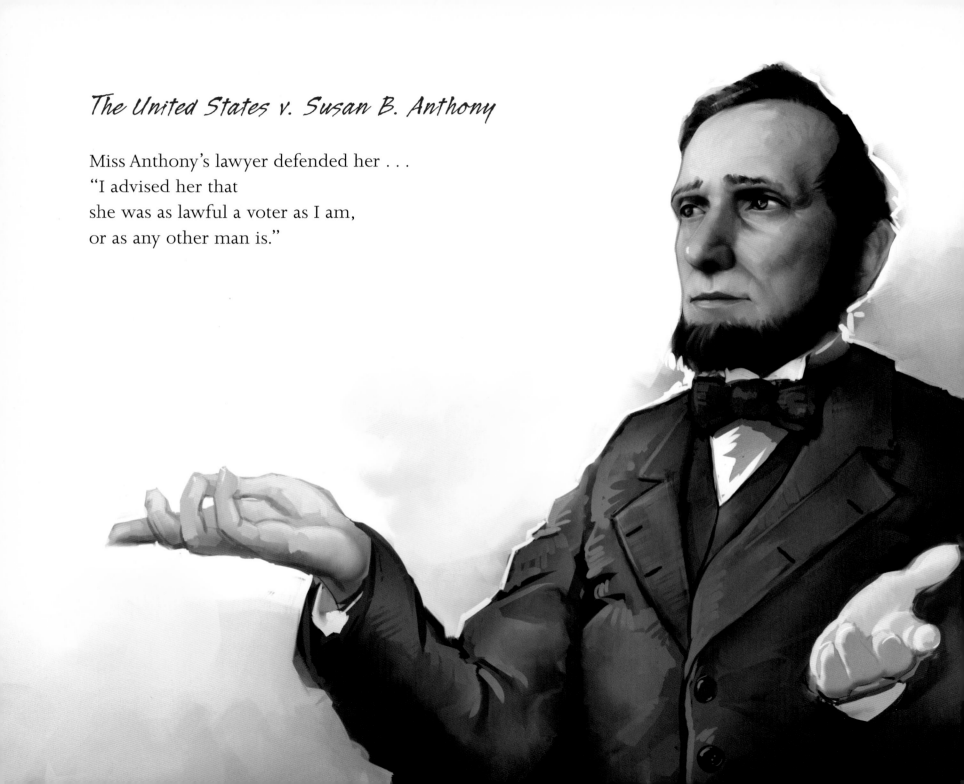

The United States v. Susan B. Anthony

Miss Anthony's lawyer defended her . . .
"I advised her that
she was as lawful a voter as I am,
or as any other man is."

The prosecutor attacked her . . .
"If she is a woman, and she voted,
and voting by women is against the law,
then she is guilty."

The judge had heard enough.
He pulled a paper from his pocket.
"The Fourteenth Amendment gives no right
to a woman to vote," he read out loud,
"and the voting by Miss Anthony
was in violation of the law."
He told the jury to find her guilty.

"The greatest outrage History ever witnessed,"
she wrote in her journal that night.

The next day, the judge asked,
"Do you have anything to say?"
Miss Anthony rose to her feet.
"Yes, Your Honor, I have many things to say . . .
You have trampled under foot
every vital principle of our government.
My natural rights,
my civil rights,
my political rights,
my judicial rights,
are all alike ignored."

The crowd inhaled.
The prosecutor tightened his lips.
The judge banged his gavel.
"The Court cannot allow the prisoner to go on!"

Her heart was on fire.
No one could stop her.
"The prisoner must sit down!"
roared the judge.
She spoke louder still,
but it was no use.

The trial was over.
Miss Anthony was found guilty.
The judge ordered her
to pay one hundred dollars plus court costs.

Outrageous.

Unbelievable.

True.

She had one more thing to say,
as a person and a citizen.
"May it please Your Honor," Miss Anthony said,
"I shall never pay a dollar of your unjust penalty."

And Susan B. Anthony never did.

By voting in the federal election in 1872, Susan Brownell Anthony hoped to claim her rights as a citizen under the Fourteenth Amendment. The new amendment was one of three adopted by Congress after the Civil War to give freedom and citizenship to black Americans. She believed the Fourteenth Amendment granted full citizenship and the vote to women, too, but many people disagreed.

Anthony knew that her vote might be challenged. The laws in New York and across the country, except in the territories of Wyoming and Utah, allowed only men to vote. Like Rosa Parks in 1955, a black woman who refused to sit in the back of the bus as the segregationist laws of Alabama required, Anthony was practicing civil disobedience. She broke an unjust law in order to try to change it. But Anthony didn't expect to be arrested. "I never dreamed of the U.S. officers prosecuting me for voting," she wrote in a letter.

After losing the trial, Anthony asked Congress to lift her hundred-dollar fine. Though she never paid or went to jail, the fine held. In 1875, the United States Supreme Court ruled that the Fourteenth Amendment did not protect the right of women to vote.

Anthony turned her attention to winning a new amendment—the women's suffrage amendment—to guarantee all American women the right to vote. Year after year, Congress refused to pass the law.

Born on February 15, 1820, to a Quaker family, Anthony fought all her life for equal rights for women. She and her friend Elizabeth Cady Stanton founded the National Woman Suffrage Association in 1869 to gain the vote for women. From her home in Rochester, New York, Anthony traveled tirelessly to spread her message. She often wore a red shawl and carried a large alligator purse. "Woman must have a purse of her own," Anthony wrote.

Many people didn't think women belonged at the voting polls, but Anthony never gave up. At her eighty-sixth birthday celebration in Washington, DC, Anthony remained determined. "Failure is impossible," she declared.

Anthony died a few weeks later on March 13, 1906. Still, the seeds she had planted grew strong. "This is winter wheat we're sowing, and other hands will harvest," Stanton had told her. Soon a new generation took up the battle. The Nineteenth Amendment was finally passed by Congress on June 4, 1919, and ratified by the states on August 18, 1920. That November, twenty-six million women cast their votes for president.

Selected Bibliography

Anthony, Susan B. *The Trial of Susan B. Anthony.* Amherst, NY: Humanity Books, 2003.

Clift, Eleanor. *Founding Sisters and the Nineteenth Amendment.* New York: John Wiley & Sons, 2003.

Gordon, Ann D. *The Trial of Susan B. Anthony.* Washington, DC: Federal Judicial Center, 2005. Retrieved Dec. 7, 2011. www.fjc.gov/history/docs/susanbanthony.pdf.

Gordon, Ann D., editor. *The Selected Papers of Elizabeth Cady Stanton & Susan B. Anthony,* vol. 2. New Brunswick, NJ: Rutgers University Press, 2000.

Harper, Ida Husted. *The Life and Work of Susan B. Anthony.* New York: Arno Press, 1969.

Lutz, Alma. *Susan B. Anthony: Rebel, Crusader, Humanitarian.* Boston: Beacon Press, 1959.

Sherr, Lynn. *Failure Is Impossible. Susan B. Anthony in Her Own Words.* New York: Times Books, 1995.

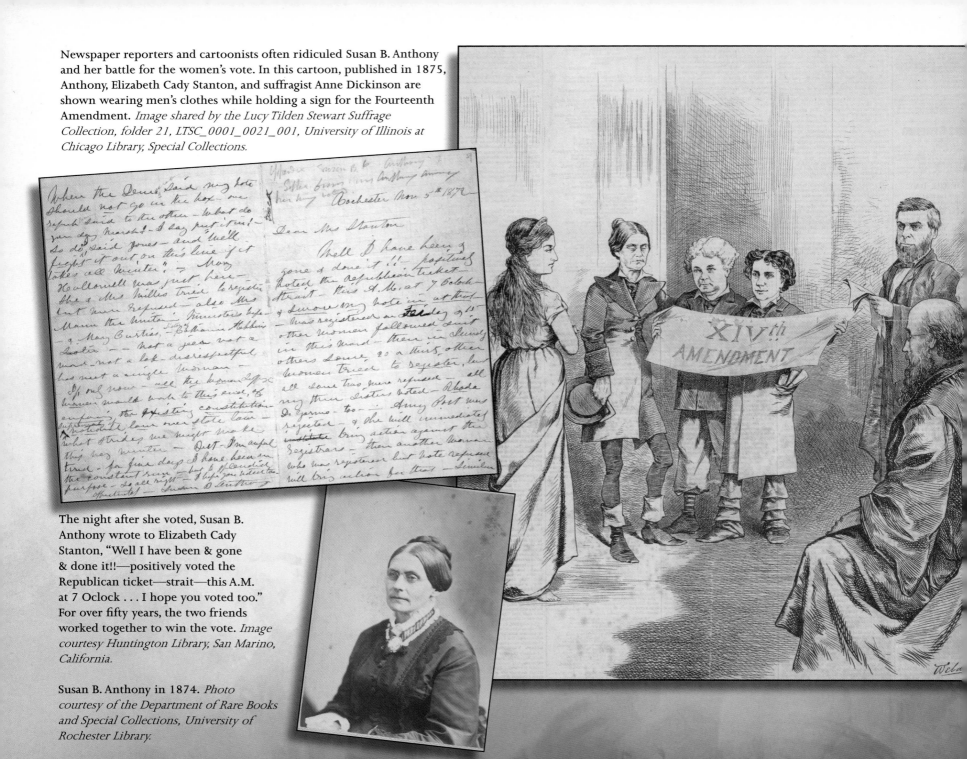

Newspaper reporters and cartoonists often ridiculed Susan B. Anthony and her battle for the women's vote. In this cartoon, published in 1875, Anthony, Elizabeth Cady Stanton, and suffragist Anne Dickinson are shown wearing men's clothes while holding a sign for the Fourteenth Amendment. *Image shared by the Lucy Tilden Stewart Suffrage Collection, folder 21, LTSC_0001_0021_001, University of Illinois at Chicago Library, Special Collections.*

The night after she voted, Susan B. Anthony wrote to Elizabeth Cady Stanton, "Well I have been & gone & done it!!—positively voted the Republican ticket—strait—this A.M. at 7 Oclock . . . I hope you voted too." For over fifty years, the two friends worked together to win the vote. *Image courtesy Huntington Library, San Marino, California.*

Susan B. Anthony in 1874. *Photo courtesy of the Department of Rare Books and Special Collections, University of Rochester Library.*